A souvenir guide

Nymans
Sussex

Claire Masset

C000148643

National Trust

Nymans,
A Triumph of Hope

In 1890 Ludwig Messel, a German émigré of Jewish descent, bought the Nymans estate in Sussex to create his dream family home.

Keen to establish himself within English society, he created one of the most fashionable gardens of the Edwardian era with a house to match.

Here Ludwig enjoyed the glory years of the pre-war era, when entertaining friends and family in splendid surroundings was the ultimate sign of success. Still today, Nymans has a warm and welcoming atmosphere that harks back to those halcyon days.

A family's creation

Ludwig, a successful banker, was the first in a line of determined and creative people and Nymans is, more than anything, the story of his family. Each generation rose up the social ladder, reaching a peak when Ludwig's great-grandson, Antony Armstrong-Jones (later Lord Snowdon), married Princess Margaret.

'Two days before the Great Storm of 1987, I became the family representative here at Nymans. Twenty-seven years later, I am thrilled that Nymans is a success with the garden as good as it would have been in the 1930s. I hope you enjoy your visit. *Floreamus!*'* (*May we flourish!*)

Alistair Buchanan, Ludwig Messel's great-grandson

Beyond their financial success, the Messels shared a love of beauty and were supremely talented in the art of creating it. In the house, furniture, antiques and paintings were skilfully arranged to produce aesthetic and intimate interiors. In the garden, exotic and rare plants were laid out to exuberant effect. Its outdoor rooms, unexpected corners and secret places, its varying moods and prospects, offered a pause from the drama of life. In the estate's ancient woodland, bathing ponds, huts and gentle landscape features were added to create fairy-tale surroundings in which the family could enjoy picnicking, fishing and swimming.

Ludwig's granddaughter, Anne Messel, once described Nymans as reflecting 'the personalities and whims of those who have trod its paths and the aspirations of its makers and improvers; mirroring a glimpse from each generation that time and growth have moulded into a harmonious whole'.

All has not been easy, however. Shortly after the end of the Second World War, in 1947, fire devastated the house leaving a romantic ruin to dominate the garden. Forty years later, the garden came close to total destruction in the Great Storm of 1987. 'Nymans' story is one of bloody mindedness,' says Alistair Buchanan, Ludwig's great-grandson. It is a triumph of hope over adversity and a story we are proud to share with you today.

Left **The Wall Garden** in early summer

Ludwig Messel, German émigré turned country gentleman

Young and ambitious, German banker Ludwig Messel came to London in the late 1860s seeking to make his fortune. By 1873 he had founded his own stockbroking firm, L. Messel & Co., which was to become one of the City's most successful brokerage houses.

Marriage and money

In 1869 Ludwig married an English lady, Annie Cussans, daughter of a former army officer, with whom he would have six children. As Ludwig's wealth grew, so too did the quality of homes he lived in. From a relatively humble dwelling in Brixton in south London, the growing family swiftly rose up the property ladder, eventually moving, in 1880, to a grand house in Westbourne Terrace, one of the most elegant avenues in Bayswater.

Ludwig was an avid collector of art and antiques, a passion which would percolate down successive generations of the Messel family. His interest in art led him to become friends with leading artists and musicians of the day, including artist Marcus Stone, lyricist W.S. Gilbert and *Punch* cartoonist Edward Linley Sambourne, whose daughter Maud married Ludwig's son Leonard.

Ludwig = Annie Cussans
(1847–1915) (1846–1920)

Leonard = Maud Sambourne
(1872–1953) (1875–1960)

Linley	Anne	Oliver
(1899–1971)	(1902–1992)	(1904–1978)

Above Ludwig and Annie Messel at Nymans

Left Ludwig and his family on the lake in the Woods; in the background is the picnic house

The perfect retreat

In 1890, Ludwig and Annie decided to find a country home for their six children. Nymans, an early Victorian house with a 240-hectare (600-acre) estate in the beautiful Sussex High Weald, was the perfect rural idyll. In the heart of 'stockbroker belt', it was the ultimate status symbol.

A new hobby

As the new owner of a large country estate, Ludwig could have left the gardening to his staff, but he developed a passion for plants, thanks in no small part to his gardening neighbours. High Beeches, just over a mile away, was home to Wilfred Loder, who was at the time developing one of Sussex's most important gardens. Ten miles away was Gravetye Manor, where William Robinson was advocating a new form of natural gardening (see page 29). With the help of his knowledgeable head gardener James Comber, Ludwig transformed Nymans into one of the great gardens of the area and a showcase for rare and exotic plants.

A gardening dynasty

Like collecting, gardening was a passion which spread down through the generations of the Messel family. As a child Ludwig's daughter Muriel would follow him and James Comber around the garden, absorbing their knowledge. Her brother Leonard and his daughter Anne both shared this passion for plants. Nowadays, keen gardener Alistair Buchanan continues the family tradition.

Above The south front of the original early 19th-century house (top) and (below) the house after Ludwig's alterations, with its large conservatory and tower

Leonard and Maud Messel, a creative couple

When Ludwig died in 1915, his eldest son Leonard inherited Nymans. At the time Leonard and his wife Maud were living at Balcombe House, a large comfortable property a short drive from his father's house. Despite resistance from Maud, Leonard persuaded his wife to move to Nymans, but only after he agreed to radical change.

Transforming the house

Maud found Nymans old-fashioned and dull, which wasn't surprising given that she grew up at the wonderfully artistic 18 Stafford Terrace in London (see panel). To her, a home should be full of charm and romance. Guided by a strong aesthetic sense, she set about transforming her new home. The result was a brilliant illusion, possessing the look and feel of an English manor house that had evolved over the centuries. Architectural historian Mary Miers described it as having 'the elusive quality of timeworn things'.

In the garden

Leonard and Maud shared an interest in their new garden, but for different reasons. Leonard was a collector; Maud an artist. While he lavished money on expanding the garden's plant collections, Maud valued flowers and shrubs for their beauty and sentimental qualities. Gardener and neighbour William Robinson summed up the dual nature of their garden when he described it as 'both instructive and beautiful'.

Creative outlets

As a young girl Maud aspired to be an artist and, although she gave up her ambitions when she married, her exquisite taste imbued everything with beauty and romance. As a skilled seamstress and needlewoman, she established the Nymans Needlework Guild, providing training and income to local women. She designed all the costumes for the local May Day celebrations. Her love of fancy dress and drama also led her to set up a local Shakespeare dramatic society.

> 'Her presence had an instant effect upon everyone who came within her orbit.'
>
> Oliver Messel on his mother Maud

The Sambourne family home

Maud's childhood home at 18 Stafford Terrace in Kensington reflects the artistic tastes of her family and is today a rare surviving example of a late 19th-century Aesthetic interior. Typical of this style was the use of Far and Middle Eastern furniture and decoration, the combination of ebonised furniture and blue-and-white ceramics, and the extensive use of natural elements as decorative features.

'My wonderful father was a born collector… He taught appreciation in the fullest sense. He was tender-hearted and generous and was dedicated to academic preservation.'

Anne Messel on her father Leonard

Opposite Maud as a young woman. This photograph clearly shows her natural stylishness and beauty, features which her daughter Anne would inherit

Left Leonard and Maud in the garden

Anne Messel, society beauty and preserver of the past

Below Anne Messel in her twenties

Below left Anne with her brothers Oliver (left) and Linley (right)

Leonard and Maud's children – Linley, Anne and Oliver – enjoyed a carefree upbringing at Nymans. For Anne though, this was not just a childhood home. Nymans was also her last home.

'It was most eccentric…laced with the whims and wisdoms of rare parents,' Anne wrote, describing her childhood. Hers was an unconventional education. She never went to school and spent much time exploring London galleries with her parents. At home, both at Nymans and at the family's London house in Lancaster Gate, she was left free to explore her own creativity.

Society beauty

A debutante in 1920, Anne was soon hailed as one of the beauties of her generation, featuring in the society pages of newspapers and magazines. As the friend and favourite of the photographer Cecil Beaton, she posed for several portraits.

Marriages and Birr Castle

In 1925 Anne married barrister Ronald Armstrong-Jones, with whom she had two children: Susan and Antony Charles Robert. The latter became Lord Snowdon, the famous photographer. After divorcing in 1935, Anne married Lawrence Michael Harvey Parsons, 6th Earl of Rosse, with whom she had two sons, William and Martin. The couple lived at Birr Castle, a grand demesne in County Offaly, Ireland, and the ancestral home of the Rosses. Like Nymans, it also has a great garden famous for its rare and exotic trees and shrubs.

A passion for the past

More than any other member of her family, Anne realised the importance of preserving the past. Without her, much of the Messel family history may well have been lost. As early as 1958, she wrote the first guidebook to Nymans; it is full of personal memories and telling detail. Anne was also the catalyst behind the creation of the Victorian Society (1958), which helps preserve Victorian and Edwardian architecture.

Nymans for the nation

Following Leonard Messel's death in February 1953, Nymans was one of the first great gardens to come to the National Trust. The early years of Trust ownership were not easy and money was short, but gradually the estate was put in order. When Maud died in 1960, Anne became the Director of the garden. After the death of her husband in 1979, Anne came back to live at Nymans, and here she stayed until her death in 1992.

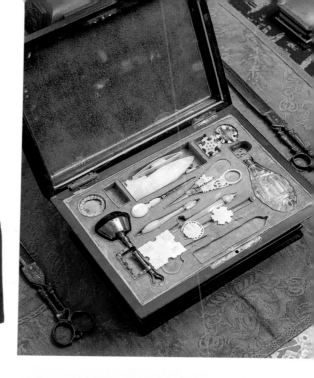

The Messel Dress Collection

This collection represents six generations of Messel women. After the death of her mother, Mary Anne Herapath, in 1895 Marion Sambourne (Maud's mother) packed away two items of clothing in memoriam. Every successive generation preserved items of their mother's clothing. Anne Messel even labelled items with personal descriptions. Attached to a floor-length wool dress is the note: 'Had a wonderful time in this dress am ashamed to say. 1941'. She gave the collection to Brighton Museum and Art Gallery in 1981.

Above Anne's workbox at Nymans – like her mother, Anne was a keen needlewoman

Left The dress Anne wore in 1941 and which she refers to in a note (see panel)

Oliver Messel, setting the stage alight

'I attempted to use every device to make as much magic as possible.'

Oliver Messel

Oliver never felt the bond with Nymans that Anne did, but his formative years here helped his creative side to flourish. He became one of the most original stage and costume designers of his day.

A creative childhood

As children, Linley, Anne and Oliver would often dress up as characters from paintings and history, no doubt encouraged by their costume-loving mother. Surrounded by art and antiques in an environment filled with creative people, Oliver developed a keen eye for beauty. With the backing of his parents, he left Eton before completing his studies to train at the Slade School of Fine Art, where he developed a romantic style influenced by the art of the 18th century.

Behind the mask

While studying art, Oliver spent his weekends making masks from papier mâché, pipe cleaners and gesso. His designs were so eye-catching that he soon started receiving commissions. Significantly, his work was noticed by the director of the *Ballets Russes*, Sergei Diaghilev, who asked him to work on masks for a production of *Zéphyr et Flore* (1925). This launched Oliver's career and by 1930 he was the most famous stage designer in Britain. A few years later, he started designing costumes and sets for films, including *Romeo and Juliet* in 1936 and *Caesar and Cleopatra*, starring Vivien Leigh, in 1945. Throughout the 1950s he worked on plays,

ballets, operas and musicals, and also created decorative schemes for shops and hotels, including a suite at London's Dorchester Hotel.

All an illusion

Oliver was a master of visual trickery. He would use everyday items – such as sweet wrappers, tin foil, string, sponges and cellophane – to create the illusion of luxury. Gold, precious stones, delicate embroidery – all were cleverly simulated. For one costume, Oliver used cream-coloured rubber to create the effect of a porcelain figure.

Life in the Caribbean

In 1966, Oliver moved to Barbados with his partner Vagn Riis-Hansen where he remained until his death in 1978. The couple transformed an old plantation house into an exquisite home and Oliver reinvented himself as an architect. With his usual theatrical flair, he built or remodelled a number of stunning beach houses.

Linley Messel

Oliver and Anne's brother, Linley Messel, never enjoyed the fame of his siblings, but he did carry on the stockbroking firm and developed a passion for farming, having studied Agriculture at Cambridge. He and his second wife, Elizabeth Downes, bought a farm near Haslemere, 30 miles west of Nymans. He was present at Nymans for the ceremony in 1954 when the gardens were formally opened to the public by the Trust.

Opposite Oliver Messel, photographed in his studio by Francis Goodman, 1945. Good-looking and charismatic, Oliver was as talented at making friends as he was at creating beauty

Left Model stage set by Oliver Messel. Art historian Sir Roy Strong once remarked that Oliver's colour palette for his stage sets was influenced by the colours in the garden at Nymans

Below *The Herbaceous Border in Summer, Nymans*, by Oliver Messel, 1930s. The painting was commissioned by his brother Linley for the boardroom of L. Messel & Co. and now hangs in the Library at Nymans

The House

'So clever a reproduction is it of a building begun in the 14th century and added to intermittently till Tudor times, that some future antiquary may well be deceived by it.'

Christopher Hussey, *Country Life*, 1932

The house you see today is much as it was when Anne, Countess of Rosse, lived here in the 1980s. Thanks to her, it reflects the many layers of history that Nymans has witnessed over its lifetime.

Anne saw Nymans as the embodiment of her parents' tastes. Still today, Nymans represents an idealised view of the English country house. So keen was Anne for things to remain as they were that when the Trust considered demolishing the ruins (see page 15), she objected, stating that they were integral to the romance of the place.

The first transformation
As soon as Ludwig bought Nymans – at the time a large but simple early Victorian house – he employed his architect brother Alfred to design a new building. Additional features, such as a tower, billiard room and large conservatory, created the feel of a gentleman's country residence. Ludwig also consulted the architect Leonard Stokes but his plans were never followed. The end result was a bit of a strange hybrid; the building never quite lived up to the potential of its original design.

From Victorian pile to medieval manor
When Leonard inherited from his father, his wife Maud insisted that she would not move to Nymans unless the house was radically transformed. He immediately commissioned the distinguished architect Norman Evill to

create a romantic, idealised country home. Maud's sketches and photos of medieval manor houses, including Great Chalfield in Wiltshire and Brede Place in Sussex, provided the starting point. Evill only lasted a year – possibly due to Maud's exacting demands – and a renowned church architect, Sir Walter Tapper, was appointed in his place.

It took five years to transform the house, but it was a resounding success. Medieval-inspired features included an entrance courtyard, arched gateway, steeply pitched roofs, a great hall and a minstrels' gallery. All combined to create the illusion of antiquity.

In the press
'Nymans is not a copy of an existing building. Rather, it is an exquisite example of pastiche – a form of invention that in literature holds an honourable place and is capable of producing works of art in their own right,' wrote architectural historian Christopher Hussey in a *Country Life* article of 1932. For a family so keen to become part of the British establishment, a lengthy feature in one of the country's most respected publications was the ultimate endorsement.

Left This view of the Forecourt Garden highlights the medieval feel which Leonard and Maud achieved in their transformation of Nymans, both in the building itself and in its surrounding garden spaces

Taste in all things

'It is the result of a charming taste directing everything, from the component and treatments of the rooms down to the choice of furniture and the arrangement of the flowers,' wrote Christopher Hussey in *Country Life*. Not only was the exterior a resounding success, the interiors reflected Maud's eye for aesthetics and the couple's love of all things antique.

The perfect illusion

Antique oak furniture, 17th-century tapestries and wall-hangings, faded rugs, flagstone floors and white-washed walls created an air of antiquity. This type of arrangement, known as the Hampton Court style, was used frequently in late Victorian and Edwardian country house interiors. But unlike many of their contemporaries trying to achieve the 'medieval manor' look, the Messels succeeded spectacularly, producing interiors which were artistic creations rather than bland period pieces.

Right With its tapestries, white-washed walls, rugs and antique furniture, the Garden Hall perfectly displays the antiquated romantic style which Maud loved so much

Opposite Mr Wells the Butler in the Forecourt Garden after the fire in 1947

Nymans at war

During the Second World War, the Great Hall was transformed into a dormitory and Nymans was home to 16 evacuees and their schoolmaster. The boys enjoyed generous supplements to their rations from the estate farm and Leonard would come and wish them goodnight every evening. After the war, he helped a few of the boys find jobs in the City.

Disaster strikes

On 19 February 1947, in the early hours of Leonard's 75th birthday, the household woke up to find Nymans on fire. It was a bitterly cold winter and staff often had to warm the frozen pipes using blowtorches – there is little doubt that one of these blowtorches caused the fire. Firemen were unable to fight the blaze, as the standpipes were frozen and they had to pump water up from a garden pond. In the morning the damage was clear: the fire had destroyed the main rooms of the south wing and half of the west range. Leonard was heartbroken;

virtually all the contents of the main rooms were gone, including his beloved botanical library (see page 23). During the blaze, Leonard made the decision to save a portrait of his mother rather than a Velázquez painting. Family always came first.

After the fire

Leonard and Maud bought and moved to Holmsted Manor, 2.5 miles away, and architect Michael Tapper, son of Sir Walter Tapper who had previously worked on the house, was appointed to restore Nymans' west range. He preserved the essence of Maud's vision, albeit on a much smaller scale, using items from the couple's house at Lancaster Gate and salvaged pieces from Nymans. Ironically, the dramatic ruins left by the fire added to the sense of romance that Maud was so keen on.

'Mr Wells the Butler and Mr Message the policeman on the other side of the house were trying to get out the furniture and it was amazing what they managed to save.'

Daphne Dengate, Maud Messel's secretary and companion

A tour of the house

The building you see today includes the surviving west range, where Anne lived until she died in 1992, the service wing (now two flats), and the ruined shell of the south range, which before the fire contained the main rooms of the house.

The Garden Link

As you enter the house, you will notice that light levels are low. This is mainly to preserve the textiles, but it also adds to the atmosphere. You get a sense of what the house would have felt like when Maud lived here; she intentionally kept the lighting low to create a romantic effect.

To the left, through the arched window, is what remains of the old Drawing Room, now a ruin. Paintings and architectural drawings hang on the walls, including two evocative views of the garden by the landscape painter Alfred Parsons. Gardeners at Nymans used the larger of the two views when restoring that part of the garden; the similarities are now clear to see.

The Garden Hall

As you listen to the clocks ticking, you might get a feel for what life was like at Nymans for Leonard and Maud. This was certainly Anne's intention. In a letter dated 1988, she wrote: 'I want the Garden Hall preserved as it is with its tapestries and all… so that the public can see what at least one of the rooms at Nymans has always been like.' The *Madonna and Child* is one of the items that survived the fire – it sits in its original position over the fireplace. Amongst the 17th-century tapestries, 16th-century oak furniture, Queen Anne-style armchairs and antique mirrors is Oliver Messel's portrait of Russian-born beauty Natalie Paley. Notice how the frame – in true Oliver style – looks like silver but a closer inspection reveals that it is actually made of folded pieces of cellophane under glass. A portrait of the famous designer, with other family photographs, stands on the piano.

'The way an atmosphere is created is remarkable.'

John Cornforth, describing the Garden Hall in *Inspiration of the Past*

Brilliant bouquets

Flowers adorn the house, as they did in
Anne's time. Anne loved flowers and would
always carry her 'nippers' with her in case
something caught her eye in the garden.
Most of the time though it was the job of
the gardener to select the flowers, though
Anne did all the flower arranging herself and
insisted the colours of the flowers should
match those of the rooms.

Left The Garden Hall door

Opposite Portrait of Anne
Messel, 1920s

The Old Staircase Hall and Link Lobby
The Dining Room Passage

The Old Staircase Hall and Link Lobby

These two connected rooms, together with the Gun Room (see page 20), appear to form a hallway along the west range. Looking at the floor in the Old Staircase Hall, you get a sense of the different eras of the house. While the stone flags are from Leonard and Maud's time, the geometric Victorian tiles, although they look more recent, actually date from Ludwig's time. And you can see where the old stair used to be before the fire; a tell-tale square slate marks the spot where the newel post was placed. Notice also the Gothic arch that separates the Old Staircase Hall and the Gun Room. It is a convincing copy of the original arch which still exists between the Garden Link and the Old Staircase Hall.

The Dining Room Passage

This passage displays some of Oliver's work. The most eye-catching picture here is his large charcoal study of the actress Merle Oberon, drawn when the actress was starring in *The Scarlet Pimpernel*. There are also portraits by Oliver of Ludwig and Leonard, as well as two designs showing plans for turning the stable block at Nymans into a villa.

Anne's home

A book entitled *The English Room* by Derry Moore and Michael Pick offers a precious record of how Nymans looked in Anne's lifetime. Photographs taken in the 1980s – such as this one – show the house when it was lived in by Anne, and were used to inspire today's layout. There are plans to re-open Anne's bedroom, which is currently used as the conservation store room. This was both her childhood bedroom and the room in which she died.

The Dining Room

Originally the upper servants' hall, this was latterly used as Anne's private dining room. The centrepiece of the room, an early 19th-century Spode supper set, allowed servants to serve and keep food warm and could be used at any time of day. The central tureen was designed for coddling eggs by simply filling the middle section with boiling water. Alternatively, the china 'egg rack' could be removed and the tureen used as a sauce dish. The remaining sections could hold meat, vegetables and other side dishes. The room features a variety of blue-and-white china, including modern Italian pieces, Japanese and Chinese export ware and Dutch Delft ware.

Left Though small, the Dining Room is a showcase of blue-and-white china, including an exceptional Spode supper set

The Gun Room
The Book Room
The Slip Passage

The Gun Room

This small area is neither a room, nor does it contain guns. Its name originates from Leonard and Maud's time when the space, then enclosed, may have been used to store guns. The eye-catching Florentine mirrors were bought by Leonard and Maud on one of their many antique-collecting holidays to Italy.

Above Florentine mirror in the Gun Room

The Book Room

It was common for country houses to have both a library and a book room. In the latter, books with a more leisurely purpose were kept. During Anne's time, this room was Lord Rosse's study. The Rosses were constantly moving between their four homes – Birr Castle, Linley Sambourne House (18 Stafford Terrace), Womersley Park and Nymans – so Anne would make sure that in each house her husband's desk was always laid out in exactly the same way.

The panelling between the Gun Room and the Book Room was acquired by Maud in the 1920s and is said to date back to the 14th century.

The Slip Passage

This small room connects the Library (see page 22) with the Gun Room and the rest of the West Passage. It features four doors: one to the garden, one to the Gun Room, one to the Stable Courtyard and one to the Cloakroom, which is curiously labelled 'dog's bathroom'. The door to the Stable Courtyard was known as the motor door as it was where cars would turn round and drop people off. The Slip Passage features Leonard's collection of walking sticks, one of which doubles up as a hoe. It must have come in handy when he was inspecting his garden!

Fabulous fans

The Book Room contains one of the many fans collected by Leonard. His collection, now in Fitzwilliam Museum in Cambridge, features over 500 fans from Europe and Asia. Anne once wrote: 'As children my brother Oliver and I were gripped and fascinated by them and our father's knowledge about them. On rare and especial occasions we had "fan evenings", reserved for a few intimate friends who were intelligent and cultured enough to appreciate them. He handled them himself and then locked them away in cabinets. The refusal to display them in the light, and handling them so rarely and carefully, is the reason for their immaculate condition today.'

Far left A view into the Book Room, where you can glimpse the striking television set decorated by Oliver for his mother Maud. Oliver designed another similar set for the Dorchester Hotel in London, where he created a penthouse suite

Left The Nymans footman used this handy post-dial to indicate when he was planning to go to the post office to send letters

The Library

Anne's favourite room, the Library is where she spent most of her time. Seated at her desk by the window, or in one of the chairs by the fireplace, in her later years she would enjoy watching guests and members of staff come and go. During the 1930s this was Linley's sitting room. Then, in the post-fire house, it became the principal sitting room, a place of entertainment and joviality.

Champagne and cocktails

From the drinks trolley by the window guests were treated to a choice of cocktails and liqueurs. Anne's favourite drink was champagne, closely followed by Dubonnet. Lord Rosse liked to mix the latter into what must have been a potent cocktail: 50 per cent Calvados, 35 per cent grapefruit juice and 15 per cent Dubonnet mixed over crushed ice and shaken for three minutes.

Left Illustration from *A Garden Flora: Trees and flowers grown in the gardens at Nymans*, published in 1918 by *Country Life*. Leonard and Muriel Messel were joint creators of this masterpiece of botanical record-keeping

Oliver's art

Two paintings – both by Oliver – take pride of place either side of the fireplace. Painted in about 1930, *Lilies* (on loan from Anne's second son William, 7th Earl of Rosse) now hangs in exactly the same spot as it would have done in Anne's time. The mirrored-glass frame, also created by Oliver, is typical of his theatrical, jewel-like style. On the other side of the fireplace is *The Herbaceous Border in Summer* (see page 11), which also dates from the 1930s when Oliver was convalescing at Nymans.

Beautiful books

The gardening books in the breakfront bookcase are a reminder of the vast botanical library that the family owned prior to the fire. In the 1920s, Nymans was home to one of the most important horticultural libraries in England, after the British Museum and the Royal Horticultural Society. The earliest books in the collection dated back to the 15th century and were written in Latin; there were also valuable early English herbals, and a rare three-volume edition of *Les Roses*, by Pierre-Joseph Redouté (known as the 'Raphael of flowers').

Today, the most significant surviving book in the collection is *A Garden Flora*, published by *Country Life* in 1918. It lists, alphabetically, over 2,000 species of plants grown at Nymans. Several copies of the book exist, but this one is significant because it features Head Gardener James Comber's annotations, recording the location and progress of each plant. In the final paragraph of the preface, Muriel Messel writes: 'I think that the garden may fitly be described as a triumph of hope. It was always full of experiments, it gave endless pleasure, and if you walk through it you will see the careful thought that was bestowed on each plant.'

Right Gardening books in the Library; before the fire in 1947, Nymans was home to one of the largest botanical libraries in the country

The Garden

Nymans is one of England's most exquisite and important gardens, famous both for its varied beauty and extensive plant collections.

Within its 13 hectares (33 acres), the garden holds stunning collections of magnolias, berberis, eucryphias, camellias and rhododendrons, together with one of the largest collections of South American plants in the United Kingdom. The sheer range of its ornamental plants – from trees and shrubs to roses, annuals, climbers and rock plants – is also impressive.

But, perhaps more than anything else, what makes Nymans so appealing is its aesthetic diversity. Its pleasing mix of formal and informal areas means that visitors can wander from one surprise to the next. Topiary gardens, manicured lawns, exquisite borders and immaculate rock and heather gardens happily co-exist with wilder areas – naturalistic lawns and flower meadows, an exuberant sub-tropical terrace and a recently planted winter garden.

True to its founders' principles, the garden is constantly evolving. 'Our focus is to keep the spirit of Nymans alive by remaining at the forefront of horticulture and making sure we are innovators in the way we carry out tasks and use plants. We're always striving for horticultural excellence,' explains Head Gardener Stephen Herrington. It's not surprising, then, that Nymans is the greenest garden within the National Trust and actively contributes to plant conservation.

Top, left to right: The June Borders at their frothy height; alliums in the June Borders; *Davidia involucrata*, also known as the handkerchief tree; magnolia flowers in the Wall Garden

'Nymans is a garden as enchanting and as full of surprises to the ignorant as to the most enlightened of highbrows. That is its great virtue.'

Anne Messel

Below, left to right: The sundial on the Tennis Lawn; topiary hedge near the house and ruins; the Temple, which offers wide views towards the woods and beyond

A garden is born

'The lawns and pleasure grounds are exceedingly well laid out. Fully stocked and planted with choice flowers and ornamental trees and shrubs. There are beautiful walks with arbours commanding splendid views.' As this extract from the Nymans sale catalogue of 1863 suggests, the garden was already in good shape when Captain John Dearden bought the estate that year. He felt no need to alter his new garden. Ludwig, who bought Nymans in 1890, was not so conservative.

A productive partnership

Five years after acquiring Nymans, Ludwig appointed a young man called James Comber as his head gardener. Both were equally passionate about plants and the pair developed a successful relationship. A horticultural expert of high standards, Comber proved the perfect man to put Ludwig's plans into action. First he tackled the Kitchen Garden, orchard, glasshouses and cutting garden.

Ludwig wanted a pinetum (page 36), so Comber obliged. Laid out in a great curve to the north of the house, it mixed varieties of pinus, thuja, cedar, juniper and cypress. To the east of the Pinetum, he planted an arboretum. Closer to the house, the old walled orchard was transformed into a cottage-style garden, with herbaceous borders edging the main path. A rose garden was planted with a mix of hybrid teas and climbers. A croquet lawn was created and the resulting escarpment was turned into a Rock Garden (page 47). Nearby a Heath Garden (page 47) was devised. Possibly the first of its kind, it was soon copied by other gardeners.

Above Head Gardener James Comber and his team

Left Ludwig in his Pinetum, one of the first spaces he created on acquiring the Nymans estate – notice how small some of the trees are

Experimentation and design

All these changes required vast amounts of money and Ludwig was happy to spend it. When it came to plants, he had little time for the ordinary and commonplace, preferring to buy rare and unusual varieties.

He and Comber experimented with plant hardiness, determined to see how tender exotics might fare in wet and windy Sussex. Every winter, plants would inevitably die, but others would thrive, which pleased Ludwig immensely. In his lifetime, he amassed a vast collection of rare trees and plants, including rhododendrons, magnolias and eucryphias. Comber and Ludwig also started the tradition of breeding new cultivars at Nymans, most notably *Eucryphia* x *nymansensis*, a beautiful white-flowering summer shrub.

But Ludwig was not just a plantsman; he was a designer too. All his purchases were planted with concern not only for their well-being, but also for their effect within a wider setting. As Shirley Nicholson writes in *Nymans: The Story of a Sussex Garden*: 'The beauty of the garden as a whole was paramount, every vista considered as part of a chain of garden pictures'.

'Ludwig Messel possessed imagination and a true artist's eye; he could play with form and colour in new and striking ways.'

Shirley Nicholson,
Nymans: The Story of a Sussex Garden

Right (above) James Comber and the impressive Monkey Puzzle tree (now gone) on the Main Lawn in front of the house

Right (below) An early 20th-century postcard of the Heath Garden

Nymans, Handcross.   895

Hard times

As the First World War approached, Ludwig's health deteriorated and he suffered from depression, partly due to growing anti-German feeling in Britain. It was to his young daughter Muriel that he turned for help in the garden.

A gifted daughter

Muriel was born ten years after her closest sibling. As a young girl in need of entertainment and companionship, she followed her father and Comber around the garden, paying close attention to their discussions. Over time she became as knowledgeable as her two unwitting tutors.

Her passion didn't go unrewarded. In her late teens, she created the borders in the Wall Garden, with the help of her father's friend William Robinson. As Ludwig became increasingly weak and despondent, she took on the management of the garden. When he died aged 68 in 1915, she was only 26. Sadly,

Above Muriel Messel with her elderly father Ludwig (and a friend) in the Woods at Nymans

Devoted head gardeners

A testament to its variety and interest, the garden at Nymans has inspired longevity from its head gardeners. James Comber stayed an incredible 60 years. Cecil Nice, who had worked with Comber for over 30 years, was appointed Head Gardener in 1953. The kitchen garden was his passion and under his leadership the sale of fruit and vegetables generated a good income. David Masters (above) took over the reins in 1980 and continued the tradition of showing Nymans-bred plants at Royal Horticultural Society shows. On his retirement in 2005, Ed Ikin took over, overseeing an extensive programme of redevelopment, including the restoration of the Rock Garden, the redesign of the Sunk and Knot Gardens, and the creation of new Mediterranean and South African beds. Ed left in 2014 and now a new chapter of the garden is beginning with the appointment of Stephen Herrington.

she succumbed to influenza in 1918, but before her death she completed one of her father's great projects: the recording of every plant in the garden.

A Garden Flora

Inspired by his friend Sir Edmund Loder, who had recently published a list of all the plants in his garden at Leonardslee, Ludwig started his own plant catalogue in 1913. As war broke out he lost hope in the project and it was far from complete when he died a year later. Muriel set herself the task of finishing the catalogue as a tribute to her father, and in 1918 *A Garden Flora* was published. With an introduction by William Robinson and illustrations by painter and garden designer Alfred Parsons, the book featured alphabetical entries for over 2,000 plants growing at Nymans.

Natural approach

Gardener and writer William Robinson, who owned nearby Gravetye Manor, advised on the borders at Nymans. His deep dislike for the overly formal gardens of the Victorian era led him to advocate 'natural gardening'. In his influential book *The Wild Garden* (1870), he recommended the use 'of perfectly hardy exotic plants under conditions where they will thrive without further care'. The Summer Borders (see page 42) demonstrate this ideal.

see page 42

Below The copy of *A Garden Flora* at Nymans is particularly interesting as it features extensive annotations by James Comber

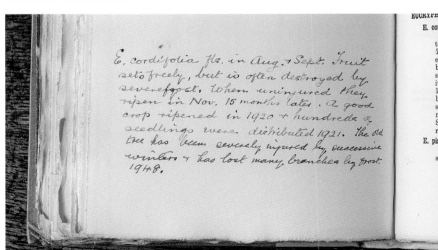

The garden under Leonard

Unlike his father, Leonard didn't have an artist's eye, but he was just as passionate about gardening. While maintaining the garden's high standards, he focused on developing Nymans' plant collections. Two men helped him in his pursuit: James Comber and his plant-hunting son, Harold.

Above Leonard and James Comber in the garden

Right (top and bottom) *Rhododendron macabeanum* and *Rhododendron lanigerum* growing at Nymans

A friend and colleague

With only a few years between them, Leonard and James Comber became firm friends. Theirs was a relationship of equals, unlike the one Ludwig had enjoyed with his head gardener. And whereas his father had amassed a large collection of rare trees and plants, Leonard focused on just a few species. He and Comber became such experts that they started exhibiting plants, particularly magnolias, camellias and rhododendrons, at the Royal Horticultural Society shows, many of which won awards. Some, such as *Rhododendron macabeanum* and *Rhododenrdon johnstoneanum*, are still growing in the garden today.

A plant-hunter from Nymans

James's son Harold was born, raised and trained at Nymans. When most of the garden staff were called up for war service, Harold – a knee injury prevented him from signing up – took charge of the glasshouses and botanical collections in the garden. He was just 17. After the war, he was sponsored to go plant collecting in South America and Tasmania and soon became a well-respected botanist and plant-hunter. Nymans was particularly proud of its plants grown from Harold's seeds and exhibited many of them over the years. His South America expedition introduced several rare Argentinian and Chilean plants – such as *Discaria discolor* and *Asteranthera ovata* – into the United Kingdom. These form the basis of Nymans' impressive Chilean collection in the Wall Garden.

Floral pursuits

Unlike her husband, Maud Messel's relationship with plants was aesthetic. The more romantic and scented the flower, the better. She was not concerned with how rare or exotic it was. Suffering from arthritis in her back, she was denied the pleasure of practical gardening (enjoyed by many Edwardian ladies), but developed a love of flower arranging. It was she who started the tradition of introducing large bouquets into the house, a practice followed by her daughter Anne and which is still maintained today. Maud also developed friendships with famous lady gardeners of her time, such as Ellen Willmott and Norah Lindsay, both of whom visited Nymans.

Messel plants

Over 30 plants are named after the Messels and members of staff at Nymans. *Magnolia* 'Anne Rosse' (right), *Camellia* 'Maud Messel' (below, right) (described as 'the world's loveliest camellia'), *Sorbus* 'Leonard Messel' and *Magnolia* x *loebneri* 'Leonard Messel' (below, left) are just a few examples. The plant-breeding tradition is still very much alive at Nymans, with new introductions such as *Eucryphia* x *nymanensis* 'Nymans Silver' and also the new fastigiate version of the handkerchief tree, *Davidia involucrata* 'Nymans Sentinel' (below, centre).

Decline and renewal

Above Gardener and authoress Vita Sackville-West (seated) with Ralph Stephenson Clarke (owner of Borde Hill) (far left), Anne Messel and Oliver Messel (right) at the opening ceremony of Nymans in 1954

Opposite A wonderfully posed photograph of Anne in the garden

Financial constraints and staff shortages caused by the Second World War put a stop to many developments in the garden. By the end of the war, the garden's glory days appeared to be over.

A gift to the Trust

When Leonard realised that none of his descendants would be able to afford the upkeep of the house and garden, he decided to bequeath Nymans to the National Trust. Both he and Trust staff believed the garden should continue acquiring new plants and remain a place of experimentation. Since the Trust's acquisition in 1953 (the year of Leonard's death), this has very much been the case. A ceremony took place on 26 March 1954, with the *grande dame* of Sissinghurst, Vita Sackville-West, officially declaring the garden open.

'Plant big, darling!'

When Maud died in 1960, Anne was appointed Garden Director. She and her second husband, Michael, Earl of Rosse, both dedicated and knowledgeable gardeners, oversaw the planting of rare trees and shrubs both at Nymans and at Birr Castle, their home in Ireland. The couple would visit Nymans, which Anne lovingly described as her 'potting shed', for weekends or over a few weeks in the summer. While Lord Rosse looked at the garden with Head Gardener Cecil Nice, Anne searched the borders, secateurs in hand, for aesthetically pleasing plants to create flower arrangements. In most things, she had a fondness for the bold and the beautiful. '"Plant big, darling," was her constant cry,' recalls Alistair Buchanan.

The tradition continues

When Anne resigned as Director in 1987, Alistair Buchanan became the family representative for Nymans. Like Ludwig and Leonard before him, Alistair had a career in finance and a passion for gardening. He spent many years looking after the Forecourt Garden (see page 50) for Anne and still cuts the topiary in the Davidia Glade (page 36). He plays an important advisory role on matters regarding the garden's development.

The Great Storm

During the Great Storm of 1987 about 500 trees were destroyed; of these almost half were in the Pinetum, and 40 were champion trees. 'It was like the Somme,' recalls Alistair Buchanan. 'We couldn't get to the garden because the road was blocked. It was five years before the garden got back to some kind of normality.' The garden team took cuttings from some of the trees which had blown over and some of the new trees are now direct descendants of the earlier ones. With hindsight it's clear that parts of the garden have actually benefited from the increased light created by the loss of tree canopy, while other areas, such as the Pinetum, are still 'recovering'.

A tour of the garden

The next pages focus on the many and varied areas of the garden. There is no set way to explore the garden; visitors are free to wander as they wish, making each journey unique.

'An English garden has to be lived in all year round; so to touch the aesthetic sense it must, like a house, embrace something deeper than a fine collection or architectural feat. It should also be a home, reflecting the personalities and whims of those that have trod its paths and the aspirations of its makers and improvers; mirroring a glimpse from each generation, that time and growth have moulded into a harmonious whole.'

Anne Messel

Right Paths are mown in the meadow next to the Pinetum, inviting visitors to explore and take in a variety of views

The Pinetum
and Davidia Glade

The Pinetum

Owning a Pinetum was the mark of a gentleman, so this was one of the first areas Leonard created, starting as early as 1892. He selected species – mainly cypresses, sequoias and cedars – for their variety of shape and colour and filled any gaps in planting with deciduous trees and shrubs such as eucryphias, hydrangeas and acers. As the plants matured, their beautiful mass merged with the wider landscape. Beyond social and aesthetic reasons, the creation of the Pinetum had a practical advantage too: it screened the house and garden from strong north-westerly winds, producing sheltered areas ideal for trialling exotic and tender plants.

When the Pinetum was opened to the public in 1955, paths were mown around and through the species-rich meadow which led to it, allowing visitors to enjoy different vistas. After the Great Storm of 1987, the Pinetum was redesigned by landscape expert Isabelle van Groeningen and the National Trust's Chief Gardens Advisor, John Sales. They framed the Wealden views with sequoias, cedars and giant redwoods. And, as Ludwig had done, they included a few deciduous trees such as acers, which helped lengthen the Pinetum's season of interest.

The Davidia Glade

This atmospheric, out-of-the-way area to the south-east of the Pinetum is a relatively recent addition. Laid out by Alistair Buchanan in the 1980s, it features topiarised box surrounding a grove of handkerchief trees (*Davidia involucrata*). Alistair still looks after his creation, a task which adds up to over 60 hours of pruning a year. 'The earth is so fertile here you have to cut the topiary twice a year,' he explains. But he does it

Viewing spots

A classical summerhouse, known as the Temple, was designed in 1904 by Ludwig's brother Alfred. Situated at the north-east corner of the Pinetum, it offered views of the Pinetum and wider countryside. Damaged by the 1987 storm, then sadly burnt to the ground, it was rebuilt and placed at the top of the meadow where you can enjoy an extensive vista. Alfred also designed the elegant viewing platform, known as the Prospect (above), which juts out over the valley near the east side of the house.

nonetheless, believing that 'when I'm pruning, I feel as though I am communicating with my great-grandfather'. The box comes from the famous topiary gardens at Packwood in Warwickshire. There are three different varieties; each grows at different rates and has different qualities, producing an attractive play of shades and shadows. It's a favourite area for children, who love playing hide-and-seek amongst the topiary.

Left and far left
A relatively recent addition to the garden, the Davidia Glade features clipped box and a grove of handkerchief trees – its effect is simple yet charming

The Top Garden

Collection', exclusively for the Plant Centre, which means visitors can take home a piece of Nymans after their visit.

Only recycled and collected water and peat-free composts are used. Because of its no-chemical policy, the nursery team relies only on biological control and environmentally friendly products. They also propagate to conserve plants, so that some of the rarer plants stay in existence and can be shared with other gardens.

The June Borders

Over 30 metres in length, the borders are the main attraction in the Top Garden. In the early 1960s the Trust's gardens advisers Graham Stuart Thomas and John Sales apparently criticised the lack of summer colour in this area of the garden. Anne promptly planted new borders 'to feature paeonies, irises, lupins and delphiniums, with clumps of roses at intervals'. The June Borders are now a graceful mix of shrubs and perennials, planted in a fairly loose, informal style.

Below Between spring and mid-summer, the June Borders feature a delicate mass of lavender-blue alliums

Left Gardeners at Nymans use harvested rainwater to water the plants in the Nursery

With its nursery and hothouses, the Top Garden was the hub where gardeners could test the hardiness of plants and create experimental hybrids.

The Nursery

Still today this is the main working area of the garden. The state-of-the-art, eco-friendly nursery supplies the garden with most of its needs. The team grows plants for new projects and makes sure there is enough stock for the following year's displays, including the splendid Summer Borders, for which over 6,000 tender annuals are grown. The Nursery also produces a select range of plants, known as 'The Nymans

The Rose Garden

When Maud created this garden in the 1920s, she planted it with herbs and old-fashioned roses. She and Leonard would obtain cuttings from friends and collect plants from the many gardens they visited in England, Scotland and on the continent. Many rare roses arrived at Nymans in this way. As a young man in the 1930s, Graham Stuart Thomas visited the garden to admire its old-fashioned roses; this may well have inspired him to become the country's leading expert on the subject.

In 1989 the garden was reworked by Isabel van Groeningen; the focus was still very much on old-fashioned roses, but with new features such as arches and pillars, as well as perennials. The idea was to create a small and intimate garden looking back to Maud Messel's romantic leanings. The Rose fountain was commissioned by Anne and Alistair Buchanan and sculpted by Vivian ap Rhys Pryce.

'A great delight to us in recent years has been the work collecting together as many of the old roses and rose species as possible'.

Leonard Messel,
Journal of the Royal Horticultural Society, 1940

Above The delicate pink bloom of *Rosa* 'Petite de Hollande' in the Rose Garden

The Wall Garden

The centrepiece of the garden is a blaze of colour, full of character and interest.

Ludwig transformed a sleepy orchard into a trial ground, both for design and plant hardiness. He introduced the marble fountain and four surrounding yews, which were clipped into eccentric chess-piece shapes; together they form the garden's iconic centrepiece. And he planted trees, lots of them, including the majestic *Davidia involucrata*, with its elegant handkerchief-like bracts, and *Magnolia campbellii*, with flowers the size of dinner plates.

The meandering paths that run through the Wall Garden invite you to wander slowly and admire the rare trees and shrubs. In spring, swathes of daffodils, primulas and snake's head fritillaries (*Fritillaria meleagris*) grow amongst the long grass creating a romantic effect, enhanced by the flowering magnolias.

The Chilean Borders

Nymans has an impressive collection of Chilean plants and many of these can be seen in the Chilean Borders on the edge of the Wall Garden. A particular highlight is the Chilean myrtle (*Luma apiculata*), a large evergreen shrub with an unusual cinnamon-coloured bark and dark purple berries in the autumn. The largest of the Chilean myrtles is what the Nymans gardening staff call a 'Comber original'; it comes from one of the seeds collected in South America by Harold Comber.

The Summer Borders

These flamboyant borders (see following pages) were designed by Muriel, with the assistance of 'natural gardener' William Robinson. Both were no doubt influenced by Gertrude Jekyll, who was famous for planting great borders of perennials artistically arranged by colour and size. They are the epitome of the Edwardian flower garden. Today this spirit lives on: blocks of flowers are planted from smallest to tallest, reaching a crescendo of dazzling colour and beauty in July and August.

Above Cosmos, marigolds and other bright annuals add zing to the Summer Borders

Left Snake's head fritillary in the Wall Garden in spring

Below The Verona marble fountain sits proudly in the middle of the Summer Borders – the perfect spot to pause and contemplate

Following pages
The Summer Borders

Recently redesigned, but in essence unchanged, the Summer Borders are based on four layers of planting. The first two consist entirely of annuals, the third is a mixture of perennials and dahlias and the fourth is perennials interspersed with grasses. Amongst the annuals, salvias are a particular highlight. Their range of colour and leaf shape, their long flowering time and relatively short height, make them ideal for the front of the border. Perennials consist, among many others, of asters, heleniums, rudbeckias and veronicastrums.

Family memorials

The Wall Garden is home to a handful of memorials including an urn dedicated to Oliver Messel (his ashes are under it). An ornate white bench commemorates the 50th anniversary of the handing over of Nymans to the National Trust and was given by members of the family of Anne, Countess of Rosse. These lend the space an air of melancholy, inviting introspection and quiet contemplation.

'The very height of Nymans is the Wall Garden. Intimate, secluded and near the house, it is perhaps the most romantic of all.'

Anne Messel

The Main Lawn and Winter Walk

While the Main Lawn is an open expanse dotted with specimen trees, shrubs and island beds, the Winter Walk is an enclosed linear walk, planted with evergreens and winter-flowering shrubs.

The Main Lawn once featured rhododendrons, magnolias, cedars and beech trees, and a huge Monkey Puzzle tree, which appears in many family photographs. Masses of camellias were added in the 1960s. During the Great Storm of 1987 many venerable trees were uprooted or subsequently died; incredibly, a cedar of Lebanon (*Cedrus libani*) which had been planted in 1850, survived. It is now a majestic punctuation mark and, in a garden where it's all-too-easy to get lost, a useful landmark.

Two of the garden's quirkiest features appear on the Main Lawn. Neatly clipped out of box, the Jasmine Basket is planted with lavish displays of red-flowered annuals in the summer so that it looks like a basket of apples. In the spring, bulbs such as narcissi and tulips fill the Ivy Bed, a circular plot surrounded by an incredible ivy hedge.

Left The witch hazel *Hamamelis* x *intermedia* 'Rubin' in the Winter Walk

Far left The Winter Walk features a variety of dogwoods planted for their colourful stems. Shown here are *Cornus sanguinea* 'Midwinter Fire', *Cornus alba* 'Kesselringii' and *Cornus sericea* 'Flaviramea'

Below Heathers and dogwoods along the Winter Walk

The Winter Walk was planted early this century by Philip Holmes, the longest serving gardener at Nymans and for the Trust. It features a great number of winter-interest plants such as hellebores, witch hazels, daphnes and pulmonarias. The fiery stems of dogwoods such as *Cornus sanguinea* 'Midwinter Fire' light up the borders at the greyest time of the year, while graceful grasses such as the bronze-hued *Deschampsia cespitosa* 'Bronzeschleier' and *Carex buchananii* give off a warm glow when backlit by the sun.

The Wild Garden

Across the road from the main garden is a secluded woodland garden well worth exploring. This area is less of a garden and more of a natural environment, similar to the Chinese and Asian woodlands where many of the plants here were originally collected by the famous botanists George Forrest and Frank Kingdon-Ward.

In Ludwig's and Leonard's time, this spot was used as a trial ground for young plants raised in the nursery from seed gathered from plant-hunting expeditions during the early 20th century. Today the Wild Garden is still home to many unusual plants, some of which are very rare in this country, such as *Pyrus glabra*, *Castanopsis sclerophylla* and *Pinus engelmannii*. Located at the top of the Garden, the Rhododendron Walk, conveniently dotted with benches and criss-crossed with paths, features many specimen trees and shrubs, including *Rhododendron thomsonii* and *Quercus acutissima*.

'The heaths have done splendidly, especially *Erica australis*, which forms huge banks of pink bells.'

Anne Messel, *A Garden Flora*

Left The Wild Garden

The Rock Garden and Heath Garden

Close to the Croquet Lawn are a number of distinct features, including a wisteria-clad pergola and an unusual mount. But most significant are the rock and heath gardens. When these were created in 1902, the former was the epitome of garden fashion and the latter cutting edge.

The Rock Garden

When the Croquet Lawn was first cut out of a slope the resulting escarpments were turned into a rock garden. Created by the famous rock landscape specialists Pulham and Sons, these areas were planted with hardy low-growing plants such as aubretias and rock roses, mixed with dwarf shrubs including cotoneaster and veronica.

In July 1914, the garden designer, painter and family friend Alfred Parsons produced a charming watercolour of the Rock Garden. About a hundred years after its creation, the garden team at Nymans used this painting as a guide when restoring this area.

The Heath Garden

Nymans' Heath Garden is one of the earliest surviving examples of its kind. No other garden had ever featured such a large and attractive area devoted to heathers. Ludwig may have been inspired by a visit to Kew Gardens where he had seen a few growing near King William's Temple. But whatever his inspiration, he knew his garden's sandy loam would be ideal for growing heathers. The ground was shaped into hillocks and divided by winding paths. About 50 varieties of winter-flowering ericas and late summer-flowering callunas were mixed with dwarf rhododendrons, dwarf mountain pines and small roses producing drifts of soft colour, ranging from milky white through to pale pink and crimson.

Since 2005, heathers with a specific Sussex connection have been added to the collection. Again, this is a first. Nymans is now home to a unique Sussex heather collection, which includes *Calluna vulgaris* 'Crowborough Beacon' and *Erica cinerea* 'Newick Lilac'. Since 2014, it has been designated a Plant Heritage Collection.

Above Alfred Parsons' watercolour of the Rock Garden; gardeners at Nymans used it as inspiration in their restoration work. It now hangs in the Garden Link (see page 16)

Left The Heath Garden

The Tennis Lawn and Sunk Garden

Bordering the Heath Garden, the Tennis Lawn features an open aspect which offers a visual and atmospheric counterpoint to its neighbour, the Sunk Garden.

The Tennis Lawn

Tennis was a popular sport in the Edwardian era and this area, as its name suggests, did indeed feature a tennis court. Assistant Head Gardener Philip Holmes remembers the garden team getting the nets out on a Friday evening for the family to play at the weekend. Nowadays the Tennis Lawn is home to two recently designed borders created by student gardeners. In keeping with the Nymans spirit, these were a chance to experiment with plant hardiness and design.

Research had shown that in the past South African plants had been trialled at Nymans and so the idea for a South African bed was born. This prairie-style bed features a vibrant mix of grasses, bulbs, perennials and annuals. Show-stopping plants, such as fiery red hot pokers (*Kniphofia*), sculptural pineapple lilies (*Eucomis*) and firework-like nerines, act as focal points amongst the grasses, which weave through the bed producing graceful movement.

Opposite the South African bed, the Mediterranean border is appropriately situated in the garden's hottest and driest spot. It boasts spiky succulents, Californian poppies (*Eschscholzia californica*) and lavenders, along with sculptural palms, agaves and yuccas.

The Sunk Garden

Sunk gardens were popular in the early 20th century and Ludwig may have been inspired by the example created at Kensington Palace in 1908, or by the Great Plat at Hestercombe in Somerset, designed by the famous gardening duo, Gertrude Jekyll and Edwin Lutyens, in 1904–8. The latter featured raised walks on three sides and stone steps at each corner leading down into the garden. The idea was that you could enjoy the plants from two different levels.

Left The South African bed

Right Bright orange Californian poppies, succulents and euphorbias in the Mediterranean Border

Here at Nymans, the Sunk Garden provided an area of intimacy within the open expanse of the lawn. Unlike most sunk gardens, this was an enclosed space, with dense evergreen plants surrounding it, and a lawn below, originally planted with roses, and from the 1930s with summer annuals. Ludwig added the great Byzantine urn made of Istrian marble, while the Italianate loggia on the east side was installed by Leonard in 1931. This lovely neoclassical structure is very much in the style of architect and garden designer Harold Peto, who was a regular visitor to Nymans.

The Sunk Garden has recently undergone a makeover. Overgrown and diseased camellias, originally planted by Anne in the 1960s, have been taken out and standard roses introduced on the perimeter of the garden. Perennials such as *Nepeta grandiflora* 'Dawn to Dusk' dotted with lavender-blue alliums adorn the island beds, creating a secluded and romantic spot.

Above The Italian Loggia in Sunk Garden

The Forecourt and Knot Garden

Bordered by hedges and walls, these two intimate areas next to the house were largely designed by Maud Messel in the 1920s. The original Forecourt – planted with roses, lavender and lilies set within a formal framework of topiary and terracotta pots and with small lawned areas intersected by paths – reflected Maud's romantic leanings and her capacity for strong design. The dovecote in the corner, another 1920s creation, was used as a garden room.

Smaller and even more secluded, the Knot Garden harked back to Tudor times (here again Maud was expressing her passion for the past) when intertwining patterns were created using low-growing herbs and clipped evergreens. To appreciate their design, knot gardens were meant to be viewed from above and, before the 1947 fire, Maud's bedroom window gave onto this small courtyard, providing the perfect vantage point.

The architectural and secluded nature of both these gardens, which were not open to the public until after Anne's death in 1992, meant they were very much like extensions of the house. They were, and indeed still are, garden 'rooms'.

Using photographs from a 1932 *Country Life* article, the Forecourt was replanted in 1992 to reflect Maud's original design. It now features standard laurels and lavender beds in the original formal arrangement. The Knot Garden was replanted in 1996 and is also true to Maud's design.

Above **Clipped evergreens and neat rows of lavender create a formal feel in the Forecourt**

Left **The view from the house towards the Forecourt**

Opposite **The ruins of the house are the perfect backdrop for large climbers, such as this magnolia**

The Terrace

Since 2005, the area in front of the house and the ruins has been the site of trial beds for exotics. Here you will find all manner of tender plants – from Sago palms (*Cycas revoluta*), bananas (*Musa basjoo*) and echiums to the weird and wonderful *Pseudopanax crassifolius* and the monster-leaved *Tetrapanax rex*. In keeping with the Messels' gardening philosophy, plant hardiness is tested to the limit in these beds. Rather than placing tender exotics in a greenhouse to overwinter, they are kept outdoors all year round, protected in winter by covers.

Climbing roses, wisterias, clematis, honeysuckle and two great magnolias (*Magnolia grandiflora* 'Goliath' and *M. grandiflora* 'Exmouth') smother the walls adding to the drama of this tropical area of the garden.

The Arboretum

Between 1902 and 1914, Ludwig Messel created the Arboretum, planting a mix of unusual and exotic trees. Linking the garden and the woodland, it is particularly attractive in the autumn, when the warm shades of acers, sweet gums (*Liquidambar styraciflua*), swamp cypress (*Taxodium distichum*) and *Nyssa sylvatica* light up the prospect. Look out for the cork oak (*Quercus suber*); mentioned in *A Garden Flora*, it dates from Ludwig's original planting.

The Woods

This ancient oak and beech woodland features majestic American redwoods, rare mosses and ferns, tinkling streams with deep pools, carpets of wild flowers and remnants of an industrial past, making it both beautiful and fascinating to explore.

Covering 99 hectares (245 acres), Nymans Woods are part of the High Weald, the most heavily wooded part of Britain and an Area of Outstanding Natural Beauty since 1983. Its varied features –valleys, sandstone outcrops, ponds and cascades – combine to create a diverse range of habitats.

Over 400 years old, Nymans' ancient woodland has been protected from development because of its steep slopes. It survives as high forest, with hazel and chestnut coppice and oak standards interspersed with a wide variety of other native species such as cherry, hazel, birch and holly. The Woods are home to many veteran trees, mainly beech and groups of ornamental conifers including the tallest tree in Sussex – a giant redwood – just topping 50 metres in 2013. From the Pinetum you can see it rise high above the canopy.

Above Nymans Woods at dawn

'Those woods are so much part of the Gardens at Nymans. They are the true English scene, the Midsummer Night's Dream of my imagination… There are lakes and ponds in the woods, the hammer-ponds of the iron founders of long ago.'

Anne Messel

Woodland walks

Our three circular walks (see inside back cover), ranging from ¾ to 2.5 miles, will help you make the most of the Woods. The longest, known as the Millennium Walk, traces the last 1,000 years of the woodland's history, highlighting areas of archaeological and natural interest. A map and guide, featuring all three walks, is available to buy.

A very special woodland

Walk through the woodland and you quickly get a sense of its variety. Narrow medieval tracks and wide grassy rides lead to sandstone ridges, pools and cascades, open meadows and clearings, all of which offer habitats for both common and rare flora and fauna.

Sandstone outcrops

Much of the woodland is designated a Site of Special Scientific Interest (SSSI) because of its rich community of birds, insects and plants, including rare and unusual mosses and ferns which thrive in the sandstone rock faces. The Woods are home to three ferns with a restricted distribution: the rare and tiny Tunbridge filmy fern (*Hymenophyllum tunbri genes*), the large and imposing royal fern (*Osmunda regalis*), and the hay-scented fern (*Dryopteris aemula*).

Deep valleys

Ghylls are a prominent feature of the Woods, as names such as Cow Ghyll, Carroty Ghyll and Foxhole Ghyll clearly demonstrate. These narrow, steep-sided valleys have a moist, warm microclimate which favours 'Atlantic' plants restricted to the Weald and the west of Britain. One example is the little-known ivy-leaved bellflower (*Wahlenbergia hederacea*). Similar to the common harebell, although much smaller, it has tiny pale-blue flowers and delicate trails of pale-green ivy-shaped leaves. The network of streams and pools within the valleys is also perfect for dragonflies, including the scarce downy emerald (*Cordulia aenea*).

Above Bluebells carpet the Woods – here a grove of oak trees – in the spring

Left The cascades and streams in the woodland are an important habitat for dragonflies

Birdlife

The woodland supports over 40 different species of birds including hawfinch, all three woodpeckers (greater spotted, lesser spotted and green), black-caps, goldcrests and nuthatches. Walk along one of the water features in the Woods and you might glimpse the blue flash of a kingfisher.

Below, clockwise from top left Nuthatch, goldcrest, greater spotted woodpecker, kingfisher

Rides and glades

Rides and glades are an important habitat for insects and butterflies, such as the silverwashed fritillary (*Argynnis paphia*) and the white admiral (*Limenitis camilla*). They're also home to an impressive array of woodland flora including orchids, anemones, wild daffodils and swathes of bluebells. Regular coppicing and periodic harvesting of over-shading trees allows light to reach the woodland floor, enhancing the beauty and biodiversity of the Woods.

A working woodland

The Woods' tranquil beauty betrays little of its industrial past, but the many historic tracks are evidence of the ways in which people have used the woodland. Holloways (sunken lanes) and tracks provided access to the ironworks, and took woodsmen to their timber and farmers to their fields. At one time the nearby village of Handcross would have been populated by people who worked mainly in the Woods.

An ancient past

Stone-age artefacts, including hand axes, flint tools and arrowheads, have been found in the Woods and suggest they were occupied by Mesolithic (10,000–5,000BC) hunter-gatherers. These transitory populations moved from one sandstone outcrop to another using them as short-term shelters. Romano-British pottery has also been found, suggesting Roman occupation.

Sources of industry

The woodland features many signs of past industry. Evidence of ironworking, for instance, as well as clay and sandstone extraction, can be seen in Jack Reeding's Wood. Many of the coppiced areas have been managed by local communities since at least the medieval period and probably much earlier; these would have produced charcoal for the iron and tanning works.

'It would have been a hive of activity – noisy and smelly.'

Chloe Bradbrooke, Lead Ranger

Ironworks

The iron industry thrived in this area between 1300 – although probably much earlier – and 1750. The geology of mixed sand and clay soils was ideal for yielding the ironstone necessary for the industry. Large pits were dug for ironstone extraction and streams were dammed to create large furnace or hammer ponds – such as Fish Pond – which powered the bellows and the forge hammers.

Brickworks

The Woods were home to a number of brickworks, such as in Brickyard Wood along Red Lane. Red Lane was so named because of the broken bricks used to help create its surface. At the works north of East Park Farm, you can still see the base of a brick kiln. These brickworks were still in use in 1794, while the pond in Brickyard Wood is said to have been created by clay extraction for bricks in the early and mid-19th century.

Marl and stone

Marl is a calcerous deposit within clay, which was used as a fertiliser in medieval times. Marl pits, such as the one in Marlpit Shaw, were dug for clay and the marl scattered over nearby fields. Sandstone quarrying was also common, as demonstrated by the large quarry in Stonepit Wood and the stone was used for buildings such as Woodlands Cottage.

Charcoal and tanning

Charcoal burning was another important industry. It was often carried out seasonally, during the spring and summer, by smallholders who bought a licence to burn. Tanning appeared in the woods in the 17th and 18th centuries and names such as Tanyard Wood give an indication of its prominence. Oak bark is a rich source of tannin, a vital ingredient in the tanning process.

Far left Ancient woodland trackway

Left An artist's impression of woodland charcoal burning

Woodland folklore

The Woods might be full of history, but they're also home to some mysterious tales.

Pookchurch Wood

This area is apparently named after a certain Reverend Pook, who allegedly preached from one of the sandstone cliffs known as Pulpit Rock to the workers as they made their way along the track from the village of Handcross to the medieval furnace by the lake. However, the name may also be a reference to Puck, an old Saxon word meaning goblin. Puck is also the nickname for the nightjar, a bird found in woodlands with a supernatural reputation because of its soundless flight.

Jack Reeding's Wood

Local legend claims that Jack Reeding was a highwayman who preyed on people travelling the old London to Brighton road. He was said to use a nearby cave as a hideout and was eventually caught and hanged outside the Red Lion Inn in Handcross in 1815. Tales are told of his ghost haunting this part of the woods; Leonard Messel claimed to have seen it.

Smugglers

This woodland, which is about the furthest one can travel in a night from the coast, may also have been used by smugglers. It's easy to imagine how the dense forest and narrow sunken tracks would have been an ideal hideout or meeting place for those bringing contraband inland from across the seas.

Right A track in the woodland

'I almost felt inclined to scream with delight this morning driving through the forest – it looked so perfectly exquisite.'

Maud Messel

The Messels and the Woods

During the Victorian and Edwardian eras, the Woods became a place of recreation for the Messels.

Pleasurable pursuits

In the late 1800s the hammer pond in Cow Wood was widened to create a lake, and a boathouse was built to house the family's two boats, one of which was called *Bollinger*, possibly after the famous champagne. A bathing hut designed by Maud was also added and the Messels would often take their tea there.

During Leonard's time, shoots were regularly organised for local gentlemen. On these occasions, Irish stew was brought down to the Keeper's Cottage from the main house in a large pot and guests would enjoy an al fresco feast after their exertions.

'I can remember him coming down the lane in the wood in a thing like a bath chair, pulled by a donkey.'

Kathleen Hallett, the gamekeeper's daughter, writing about Ludwig Messel

Above **A lady (possibly Maud) in the Woods**

Left **Ludwig on the Lake**

The house in the Woods

Old House was Lord Snowdon's unusual country retreat on the estate which he inherited from his uncle, Oliver Messel. The building, originally the Iron Master's house, was in ruins when he took possession of it in 1978, but he sensed its potential. Lord Snowdon didn't like the garden at Nymans; it lacked 'any streams, ponds or lakes, which I find essential in any garden'. Here, though, he could create his perfect garden. He dug over the lake near Old House and created an oriental-style jetty based on one he saw in Bangkok; he introduced geese too, stating they looked just like swans from a distance (and were much cheaper!). Near the house he added a gypsy caravan, an ornate folly and a reflective pool. The folly was mere artifice: a clever *trompe l'oeil* made of rendered breeze blocks. One journalist described it as 'a witty construction of elaborate fakery'. Snowdon's response was, 'the definition of a true folly is that if it is of any use at all, it is no longer a folly, and mine had absolutely no function whatsoever'.

Gardening reaches the Woods

The Messels did much to change the look and feel of the Woods, making them more ornamental in places. The lake and other areas of woodland were planted extensively with rhododendrons. The Conifer Avenue was created in the late 19th century; most of the trees here are coastal redwoods (*Sequoia sempervirens*), but there is a variety of firs too. Arguably the most beautiful man-made addition to the Woods are the cascades – pools created from the natural streams dammed to form a series of steps over which water gently flows. The story goes that after the First World War, Leonard, wanting to offer work to demobilised servicemen, commissioned the men to create these water features.

Above **Muriel near the Gatekeeper's Cottage**

Below **A shoot in the Woods**

The woodland today

The Woods are looked after by the ranger team and woodland volunteers. While working to enhance wildlife habitats and keeping age-old management techniques alive, we also encourage people to enjoy the Woods.

Messel features

Many of the Messel family's contributions to the Woods survive, including the historic Conifer Avenue and the delightful cascades. Sadly, other elements, such as the boathouse and bathing hut, have been lost. Certain species that were planted by the family were, unbeknownst to them, either invasive or detrimental to the environment. *Rhodondenron ponticum* – so popular in the Victorian and Edwardian eras – outgrows everything around it. It now has to be controlled so that our impressive array of native wildflowers can thrive. The conifer plantations

have been harvested and the areas allowed to naturally regenerate; this encourages native species such as birch, ash, beech and oak.

Coppicing

In Bluebell or Pookchurch Wood hazel is coppiced on a five- to ten-year cycle. The cuttings are used as supports in the glorious Summer Borders. This length of rotation allows a regular food supply for wildlife such as dormice and the increased light that coppicing produces is ideal for wildflowers, such as bluebells, daffodils, primroses, wood anemones and dog violets.

Traditional crafts

Woodland crafts are being revived to make a range of hand-made, rustic and seasonal products. Using coppice materials, volunteers make pea-sticks, bean-poles, hurdles, plant labels and bird boxes, which are sold in the special woodland crafts area of the shop.

Above This bridge was rebuilt in 2014 by volunteers using oak from the Woods; it's now appropriately called Volunteers' Bridge

Left Visitor having a go at woodland crafts

Opposite Every summer volunteers work this traditional kiln to produce charcoal for barbecues

Demonstrations are sometimes given by the National Trust team on how to use traditional timber tools such as billhooks and shaving horses (a combined vice and workbench).

Timber products

Volunteers use timber from the estate to make steps, railings, boardwalks, benches, bridges and smallish structures such as bird hides within the woodland. Most of the timber comes either from trees which have had to be felled for safety reasons or as a by-product of conservation work such as glade creation.

Charcoal production

A traditional metal ring-kiln is worked by volunteers through the summer to produce charcoal for barbecues. 'We don't fell trees solely for making charcoal,' explains Chloe. 'It's all by-products from other conservation jobs.' There's a technique to placing the wood in the kiln: 'It's all about the first layer – you have to make tunnels so that you have air going all the way through and then you pack it as tightly as possible as you go up.'

> 'We have to conserve both the ecology and history.'
> Chloe Bradbrooke,
> Lead Ranger

Eyecatchers

Look out for three beautifully crafted sculptures within the woods. One features a toad, stag beetle and some woodlice to illustrate decay in a large beech log. Another one shows a kingfisher perched by the lake with sticklebacks in the reeds; a third is a striking representation of two owls high in the canopy.

Nymans Today

The spirit of Nymans is as strong today as it was when Ludwig created his dream home.

Warm and welcoming, sometimes quirky but always delightful, Nymans is still infused with the Messel family's legacy of experimentation and creativity. The atmosphere is one of relaxed enjoyment, very much in keeping with its origins.

True to its creators' aspirations, the garden is still evolving and appealing in every season. New areas are created and old ones rejuvenated, always with a focus on horticultural excellence, conservation and innovation.

In the house, a small gallery now hosts seasonal exhibitions, while the second-hand bookshop and plant centre are popular destinations at the end of the day. Outdoors, you can join one of our regular guided walks and talks in the garden and woods, enjoy a woodwork display, or take part in a range of woodland activities. And if you want to know more about the plants in the garden or the items in the house, don't hesitate to ask. Now, as before, the appeal of Nymans lies in its people – their passion, dedication and love for this wonderful place.

'Here love and beauty dwell.'
Eric Parker, brother-in-law to Leonard Messel

Below Spring gardening in the Wall Garden